MW01119201

10 Easy Steps
to
Self-Publish
Your Book
For Free

Faye Menczer Ascher

ISBN: 10-153491920
ISBN-13:978-15349119129

In Gratitude

This book is dedicated to the wonderful computer staff at the West Bloomfield Library, Alexis, Gillian and Courtney who patiently gave me hours and hours of tutoring so I could learn to use Microsoft Word on my Mac laptop.

To the technicians at CreateSpace around the globe who patiently answered my myriad questions day and night.

To the Apple Store instructors at Twelve Oaks Mall, especially, Jim, who held my hand as I baby stepped through learning to use my Apple computer over the past two years.

Faye Menczer Ascher

CONTENTS

ACKNOWLEDGMENTS

Michael Menczer
for his marvelous computer skills
and help in editing this book

Al Ascher
for his constant love and support

10 Easy Steps to Self-Publish Your Book

The 10 Easy Steps

1. Go to CS

2. Log into your account

3. Start your title

4. Start your new project

5. Title information

6. ISBN

7. Interior Set up: Upload your book

8. Create your cover

9. Launch reviewer

10. Review your book

Why I Wrote This Book

Dear Reader,

I started writing children's picture books in February 2015 when my only two grandchildren moved to England and there was not only a hole in my heart but 15 hours a week when I was not baby-sitting. I wanted to fill this time with something that would keep the children close to me and be interesting and worthwhile. I decided to write stories for the children, who were 3 and 7. The books for them needed to be colorful and interesting. Neither a writer, nor an artist, my new life began. There was so much to learn, and the learning was very exciting and rewarding.

I have now self-published ten various kinds of fiction and non-fiction books.

Writing and publishing has become such a passion, I want to spread the joy of authoring and producing to the world. CreateSpace (**CS**) and Amazon are the miracle businesses that make it possible for everyone to be a published wordsmith.

The joy of giving birth to a book, holding your own volume in your hands, seeing it on the book shelf, is quite amazing.

You might also want to know that my computer skills were modest when I began and I spent more time at the Apple Store taking training with their wonderful staff than I did writing. I needed to learn so much, especially because picture books were such a complicated way to begin. I also knew nothing of CreateSpace (**CS**) or self-publishing and I created the first books using a photo album program called SnapFish.

The first books I did, a year ago, were photo albums with my stories and pictures. It made my work twice as hard. The creating of each page, needing to save them as photos, so I could put them in the computer album was a lot of work. But I learned about the computer and how to create a book.

This is the time to apologize for the poor quality of any of the images and screen shots in this book. I have not perfected my technical ability and am still working on my graphic skills, but I have come a long way.

Also, to keep the price lower, I am publishing in black and white. This has added to the visibility of some copied images which are dark on dark and I realize hard to see. I have tried to make improvements where I could.

About six months ago someone told me about **CS** and producing books flowed more smoothly. I still have a lot more to learn and continue to have dozens of questions.

Once I learned the **CS** phone number, it was like the solution to every problem was a phone call away. Now that I am publishing with **CS**, it is just so much faster to turn out books. My family is quite amazed at what I have accomplished and so am I.

I am writing this "How to" tome to help make book creation easier for everyone, and at the same time to share my passion for producing physical paperbacks. You will be made aware of how many personal writing/printing mistakes were made, by yours truly, and what to do to prevent making them yourself.

My first CreateSpace book was published in March 2016. It is now July 2016 and this is my 10th book. If I can do it, so can you!!!

Disclaimer:

I am not employed by CreateSpace and receive no compensation for my endorsement from CreateSpace (CS).

Faye Menczer Ascher

For Whom is This Book Written?

This book is primarily intended for the person who wishes to publish a personal book, or leave a physical book legacy for friends and family. My audience is the person who considers the process a success when they can hold a soft cover copy of their book in their hands. The goal of this book, is to walk you through the steps needed to go to <u>CreateSpace.Com</u> (**CS**) and publish your book.

This book can also be used by the person who has a dream of writing a best seller and making a fortune from a novel (or other type of book) but that is not the primary purpose for which it is written. If you want to create an authoring business, this book will get you started in having a book published, but it does not deal with the myriad of other issues in promotion and marketing that are necessary to create a best seller.

In simple language, with many screen shots, this book will walk you through the steps to publish a physical book on CreateSpace.com. CreateSpace (**CS**) is a division of Amazon. It is an easy process with lots of support available, especially a 24/7 phone line.

The phone technicians are wonderful and very helpful and consider no question too simple, no matter how many times you have to ask. They also encourage you to call back if you need more help. If necessary, they will walk you through every step of the process. They want you to succeed and so do I.

Although this guide is designed for the beginner, who has limited computer skills, it will also benefit the computer whiz.

The hardest part of publishing is not the actual publishing process, that is pretty basic, and there is a lot of help. The process of writing, editing and completing the manuscript is the hardest part. But if the project is mainly for your personal use or as a memento for your family, I urge you to not spend too much time on the details of the writing, the struggling over every word, the hours and hours of editing and sweating to make it perfect.

It is suggested you get it written and completed. Then publish when it looks good enough, don't wait for perfect. After you see the physical book, it will be much clearer what changes are necessary and what is good enough. You will save yourself a lot of time and anguish and remember, you can always resubmit.

The ability to resubmit multiple times is one of the most wonderful things about working with CreateSpace (**CS**). You are given the opportunity to review your work, with the issues to be cleaned up clearly marked and have time to correct the problems. You can do this even after you have seen a print copy. You get to preview your book, for as long as you need, actually seeing how it looks before you have it printed and even after it is printed, you can still make changes.

Once you see your actual book, hold it in your hands, read it, you will have a much better idea of the things you might want to change, or errors you missed. On a recent book, I did not realize until I held the book in my hands that I had misspelled my email address on the back cover. It was a typo no one caught. I was able to resubmit the cover and no one saw the error but me.

The cost of the printed book, is downright cheap, to you the author, usually less than $5. If the physical book needs corrections and you need to order a 2nd proof it doesn't break the bank.

NOTE: I use Microsoft Word for Mac 2016, so some of my directions maybe slightly different for whatever computer version you have. If you have a PC computer, you can do more things more easily, because you are using Word on a Microsoft based computer. The Mac version has some limitations.

IMPORTANT

The information in this book is based on things I personally have done in publishing my books. The information was accurate at the time this book was written. If it no longer is accurate at the time you use this book, I encourage you to call CreateSpace (**CS**) and have them help you.

PHONE NUMBER
for CreateSpace 1-866-356-2154

Do I Need to be a Computer Whiz?

If you can get to CreateSpace.com by typing it into the search bar of your computer and you can type your book on the computer, you have the two basic skills needed to self-publish on line.

Type Createspace.com in search bar

What If This Book is Too Simple?

For those of you with good computer skills and understanding, I apologize if it is too simple, too elementary, too basic and too repetitive. I am writing it for someone, like me, who still needs all the help they can get and hand holding.

Chapter 1:
What is Self-Publishing?

Self-publishing means you are in control and handling all of the aspects of the writing process. You write the manuscript, submit the work to be published, create your own cover, insert your own art work, or you pay someone to do these things. You are the editor, all errors and problems are yours. But **CS** is there to help you both to identify the problems and help solve them.

Self-publishing gives you creative control. You don't need permission from anyone to write what you want to write. You control the length, the title, the cover, all of it.

It is much faster to self-publish. You can preview your book in about 24 hours after you submit your manuscript.

It also means you have all the work of getting your work finished, and ready to publish. You may have to learn some new skills. There will be mistakes and some frustration or stress. But this can be the most wonderful adventure for you as it still is for me. The process is completed when you have a finished physical book that is in print, that you can put on your book shelf.

Although it is possible to make a fortune from a best selling book, it is not likely. This is true with all published books, self-published or from a well-known publishing house. Most authors make $2 a book. As an independent author you get to set your own price and can control all expenses.

Another bonus of self-publishing is that it is Print on Demand (POD). A book is printed when ordered. No one has stacks of books sitting around. There are no minimums. You can order one book or 10 books, or whatever you want. But you don't need to order any minimum number.

The advent of Print on Demand is one reason companies like Amazon are able to create your books at no cost to you. It has expanded the publishing business.

Chapter 2: Things to Know

There are several things to know before you can publish and a few decisions to make. These topics will be covered in more detail, with all the "how to" steps in later chapters.

Book Layout:

Once you have completed the writing, and before you can submit your book it has to meet **CS'**s requirements. They say they will accept a .doc or .docx file, which is what most documents are saved as, but if you have a lot of art or photos or clipart, it may not transfer well to the printing process unless it is a .PDF. It is very easy to change your manuscript from a .doc or .docx to a .PDF and I will give you three simple steps.

Opening Your Book:

English books begin with the first page on the right hand side and the page on the left is blank. You want your book to look like that also.

When you look over your completed book make sure that the first page is on the right and the left page is blank.

Take a look at books in your library and see how authors have put their pages together and then copy that format.

Microsoft Word:

CS is especially Microsoft (Ms) Word friendly and the **CS** technicians know all there is to know to help you. They may have some difficulty in advising you with Mac Pages because they are much less familiar with Apple. For those of you using Apple Pages there is a phone number for Apple help at the end of the book.

18

In preparing this book, I felt it was important for me to be proficient in MS Word. I bought "Office 365 for Mac" from Microsoft. It gave me MS Word for my Apple computer, which I did not have before. This book was written on Word 2016 for Mac. All my MS Word documents save as a .docx. Your versions of Word maybe different.

Book Trim Size:

The trim size is the physical measurement of your book. If you were to take a ruler to the cover, that is the trim size. The standard page size when typing on your computer is 8.5" X 11". If you choose to use this size for your book, there is no conversion necessary. A smaller size will probably require some reconfiguring of the original manuscript.

If you are at the beginning of writing, select the

final trim size you want and do your typing on that size template.

If you like to experiment, and want a smaller sized paperback you might prefer the 5" X 8" or the 6" X 9" size. **CS** gives you a lot of sizes.

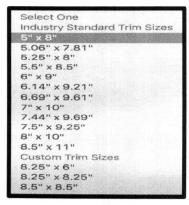

Select a size that is on your computer and acceptable to CS. Look in your library for paperback sizes. Here is a list from **CS**

Number of Pages: CS requires a minimum of 24 pages, including your title page, your dedication page, all interior pages. If you can't reach 24 you can add some pages at the end with the word "Notes." I believe the maximum number of pages is 600. There are some restrictions on the number of blank pages.

Black and White or Full Color:

My picture books for children are full color. The journals and "How to" books, like this one, are black and white. Black and white books are less expensive to produce and price. But, even full color books are reasonable. A 300 page full color book is less than $25. If you are only

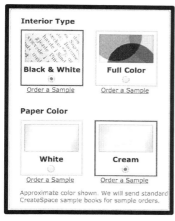

ordering a few books, and you want your color photos or pictures accurately represented, you may choose to go full color.

If your book, like this one, originally had color images, but is produced as a black and white, there will be no color. All the color will be converted to black and white. If you have even a little color, red circles, or blue lines, the book is considered full color and will be priced accordingly. **CS** does not seem to quantify how much color is used. Here is the form **CS** uses for you to make your color choices

Your Browser:

I just looked up the difference between a browser and a search engine so I can call these by their correct names. Some browsers are Firefox, Google Chrome, Safari. Search engines include Google, Bing and Yahoo.

CS works best with Google Chrome or Firefox browsers. My primary browser is Safari and that causes some problems. Most computers give you a choice of search engines, or they are free to download. Any of these browsers have detailed instructions for downloading.

Artwork or Photos:

When including artwork, photos, or non- text of any kind **CS** requires that the art be a minimum resolution or quality of 300 pixels. You should use the best resolution and largest size copy of your photos as you can. Very often **CS** will tell you your art is not of good enough resolution. My personal experience has been, although I always get this warning, and did with this book also, the actual print book looks fine, and even on the **CS** Previewer, it looks just fine. I usually ignore this issue, and wait until I see the actual book. I have not yet had a problem, even with my full color children's books, where the color and resolution is very important. I suggest if you get a warning you contact CS and discuss it with them.

To Bleed or Not to Bleed:
What is Bleed?

The bleed is how far the picture extends to the edge of the page. A full bleed means the picture goes to all edges with no margins. No bleed pages the art ends before the edge of the page. **CS** will not print book if the bleed margins are not correct.

If your book is primarily text, select a "non-bleed" format. A non-bleed has a white margin around the page, which is what you want for most non- picture books. Here is a sample from two of my books. The picture book on the left is full bleed, the one on the right is not. It has white margins all around the page. Books with no bleed are easier to set up.

Bleed   No Bleed

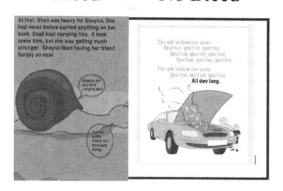

Bleed books have very specific margin requirements that can get tricky. So if you have full bleed, be sure to review carefully margin requirements. Every picture book I published had margin issues and I had to resubmit several times. Fortunately, it was only time consuming and **CS** was very helpful.

Picture Books:

Not wishing to discourage anyone, but picture books with lots of images are much harder to assemble and get ready to produce and get looking just the way you want than to look.

Text only is much easier. The issue is not publishing, that is pretty standard, but creating picture books can be more labor intensive.

Legal Issues:

When I first started doing my SnapFish books only for my family, with no thought of commercial selling of the books, I freely used art from the internet. Now that my books are for sale, I am very careful about the legal issues. Any artwork, or any copyright material you are not allowed to use without permission. All of your work must be yours, licensed to you, be public domain, free to any user, or your own art work. There are a lot of public domain sites with free art. At the end of the book I have listed some useful websites

E-books:

E-books are books available on line through an

Amazon Kindle or other on line publishers. They are very popular, but not something covered in "*10 Easy Steps to Self-Publish Your Book*". Most how to self-publish books like this start with publishing E-books. I think what you want is a physical entity, a real book, for yourself and loved ones. Most of my books are both soft cover and E-books. I find it easier to do the physical book first then do the E-book, but most independent authors seem to prefer to do it the other way around. This book does not cover how to publish an E-book. It is only dealing with publishing a physical soft cover book.

Kindle Direct Publishing (KDP) has a tool

provided by Amazon to help you create an on-line book, if you want more information on how to do a Kindle book go to Amazon or KDP.com.

POD:

Print-on demand. **CS** is a POD. A book is only printed after it is ordered. So, no one, including you, has to order a minimum number of books, or has to have a stack of books sitting in their living room. It also is why you can make changes to your book, without costing anything.

With POD there are no piles of books, no upfront printing costs, no warehousing or inventory management for you or **CS**, no shipping, or packaging by you. POD is what makes this self-publishing so wonderful.

It is free to self-publish on CS and they take a share of the cost of the book anyone buys. The technology makes it quite amazing that you can create a real, physical, soft cover book for no money.

How is the Quality
of the Paperback Book?

It is exactly like any paperback you find in a library or a bookstore. **CS** calls it library quality. At one time it looked cheap, but not any longer. Great quality.

Can I get a hardcover book?

CS does not do hardcover. There are companies that will publish a hardcover book, Ingram Spark, or Lulu are publishing houses that do hardcovers, embossing, and other special types of printing, and are POD.

Free Book Templates:

A template is a pre-formatted starting point to make it easier to organize the sections of your book and be sure they are correctly built to meet all of **CS**'s requirements. **CS** provides two template choices, a Basic Blank and a Formatted.

My Personal Experience with the Templates

Wanting to get more experience with **CS** templates, I used the Basic Blank Template for one of my journal books. It went very easily and there were no problems. It had no illustrations or graphics, only text.

I attempted to use the Formatted Template for *The 10 Easy Steps,* after it was completely written. The cutting and pasting process was time consuming and not efficient.

My next book I will start with the Formatted Template and do the writing within the template.

It might help you to know that **CS** is most compatible with Google Chrome or Firefox browsers. If you use Safari, or some other browser, you may have some trouble with the templates and the uploading of your file.

The first time I tried the Basic Template with

*The 10 Easy Step*s, the many screen shots were all missing. I am sure you can imagine my distress.

CS explained the issues were twofold, first was my Apple Safari browser, the second was '.docx'. I switched to Google Chrome and converted to a '.pdf' and it cured the problem. All the images came through.

CS FORMATTED TEMPLATE

This is the **CS** Formatted Template" at 50% view to show several pages. I know it is hard to read, but gives you the idea.

The 12 page titles are: Title, Copyright, Dedication, *a blank page*, Table of Contents, *a blank page*, Acknowledgments, *a blank page*, Chapter 1, Chapter 2, Chapter 3, etc.

The complete template outlines your whole book. If you are beginning your book the Formatted Template is a good resource for you. You type the info right on the page or copy and paste your info onto each page. You do have to download the template and open it from your downloaded file. It is a good idea to save a copy of the template on your desktop for future reference.

On the next page is another screen shot that is easier to read. it only shows 4 pages.

Book
Title

AUTHOR NAME

Copyright © 2012 Author Name
All rights reserved.
ISBN:
ISBN-13:

CONTENTS

This is the **CS** Basic Blank Template." You see it is unmarked. What it says in the small print is:

This is the 8.5 x 11 Basic Template. Paste your manuscript into this template or simply start typing. Delete this text prior to use.

"This is the 8.5 x 11 Basic Template. Paste your manuscript into this template or simply start typing. Delete this text prior to use."

CS Can Not Screen Share:

Screen sharing is when you allow an outsider, like **CS**, access to your computer to see your screen and see what you are doing. Sometimes they can take control and make the changes and sometimes they can only see it, but not make any changes. **CS** cannot "screen share," or see what you are seeing on your screen. But, they can go behind the scenes from their end and see where you are in your progress to complete your book. When you describe the problem, they know their product very well, and can usually figure out the help you need.

Your Set-Up Progress Report:

While you are working on your projects **CS** has various progress reports to help you stay focused on the task at hand. To the left of your **CS** screen there is a set-up progress column letting you know where you are with your set-up process. There is also a strip at the top of the page when you log in on your Project Homepage. You can go to the next publishing step from either of these forms.

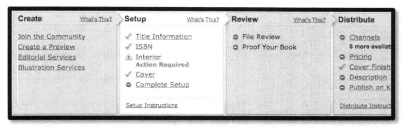

Chapter 3: Intro to Book Covers

The book cover includes the front and back cover and the spine (if any). A book under 50 pages is not thick enough to need a spine, but I like to leave a space for it on my picture books. You can use the **CS** templates and **Cover Creator** or design your own covers. I have used both. **CS** requires that all the covers be full bleed. A book with cream color interior pages will be slightly thicker than one with white pages. Book thickness and number of pages is important in determining margins for your cover. The **CS** Template handles all of these issues.

When using MS Word for my nonfiction books, like this one, I used the **CS** Cover Creator. I used their images and my own. The cover templates offer several choices and good results. When building my picture books on Apple

36

Pages I created my own covers and did not use templates.

With all covers that I created for the picture books I designed the front and back pages separately and copied and pasted them into the single cover page.

You can see it on this cover. There are two individual pages that were copied and pasted into the single sheet. You can also see the narrow white area for the spine.

Matte or Glossy:

This is your choice. Pick the one you prefer. You can ask to see a sample. I like glossy for all my book covers.

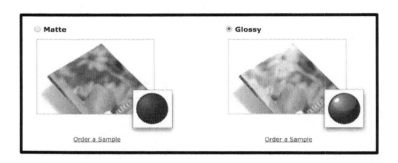

CS Cover Creator Program

The **CS** Cover Creator program offers a lot of choices in the looks of the cover and available art. But it is also very rigid and you cannot make very many changes. You can't change font, or text size, or page placement.

Details of how to use the CS Cover Creator program are in Chapter 6.

Cover Size:

You will need to submit your front and back cover on a single sheet, not two. If you have anything written on your book spine that will also need to be on the same sheet. For all books the cover size must include space for the spine and the gutter.

The gutter is the inside margin where the book is glued together.

With a trim size of 5" x 8" , with up to 200 pages, the book's cover had to be formatted on a page that was 10.56" x 8.26". This includes the front and back and spine, and makes sure the cover is full bleed.

This screenshot is the cover I submitted for my 8.5" x 11" "Camel" book. It is a single page with the front and back covers and white space for the spine. The cover template had to be 17.26" x 11.26".

It is best to ask **CS** about the requirements for your size book.

Cover Design and Artwork:

You can use a wide variety of public domain art, or a family photo, or your own art to design your cover artwork and text. This book will not teach how to use the computer to create the cover, but if you select a CS template and Cover Creator, they have a wide variety of pictures and choices from which to choose.

Here are only 6 choices from 5 pages of themes.

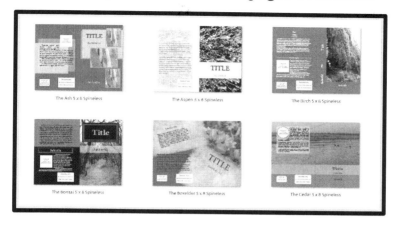

CS Image Gallery:

The screenshot on the next page shows a listing of some of the choices and topics for the over 2000 free art images you can use in your book. You can also upload your own artwork or photos to use in the Cover Creator. These images are available to use for free within your book by copying and pasting. CS does not give you permission to download all the photo files to your computer.

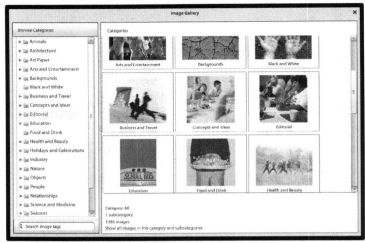

ISBN:

International Standard Book Number is the number the book industry uses to identify a book in their computer system. They are not required for personal publishing, but they are assigned for free by **CS** and look so nice on the back of the book. **CS** does all the work so why not?

Once assigned the ISBN cannot be changed.

ISBN

What to do on this page: An <u>ISBN</u> is required to publish an
right for you.

* You can skip this section if you haven't decided which ISBN
can publish your book. <u>Return to your Project Homepage</u>

Choose an ISBN option for your book:

○ **Free CreateSpace-Assigned ISBN**

　 can assign an ISBN to your book at no charge.

○ **Custom Universal ISBN**

　 Set a custom imprint while keeping your distribution

○ **Provide Your Own ISBN**

　 If you have an ISBN that you purchased from Bowke
　 publish your book through CreateSpace. You must al

Chapter 4: Book Readiness

Saving as a '.PDF':

Here are the 3 simples steps to convert your book file from a '.doc', or '.docx' to a '.pdf.'

1. File

2. Save As... (Give it a new name)

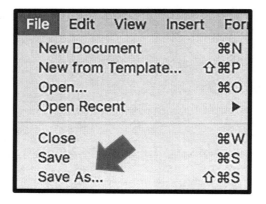

3. Select .pdf in file format box.

This FILE FORMAT is at the bottom of your
screen. It will say:

> Word document in the search box. You
> need to click on the arrows on the right
> side of the search box.

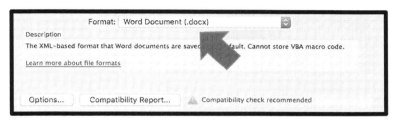

When you click on the blue arrows above you
will see this next screen. Click PDF.

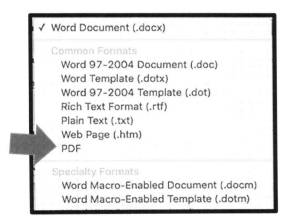

Have you left adequate margins?

A half inch margin on all four sides, for a non-bleed book with less than 300 pages is acceptable. **CS**'margin requirements depend on the number of pages and whether it is full bleed. The thicker the book, the more space is needed for the gutter.

Be careful that art and photos are not too close to the outside margin. This can be a serious issue.

Naming Your Files:

Do you remember what you called the final book file you want to publish and where you saved it on your computer?

It is suggested you write down the exact title of the file you want to publish on a piece of paper and record where it is saved on your computer (desktop, documents, other). I stress this because I had a lot of trouble when I kept uploading the wrong files, because I had so many files with similar names.

Open a CS Account

You have to have a **CS** account to publish. You can do this at any time during the writing process and just have it ready when you are ready to publish. There is no charge to open an account and it is very clear what to do. In the screen shot below they give you two places to SIGN UP. You will be given a **CS** account number. Every time you call **CS** they will ask you for this number so keep it handy. I call so often, that I keep the phone number and ID taped to my computer. Your number ID is also listed on your Member Dashboard.

TIP: To get back to your Member Dashboard, click on the **CS** logo on the upper left of your screen.

CS Help:

CS provides a lot of valuable information to help your publishing process be as easy and smooth as possible. Every screen offers expanded help and suggestions. You are encouraged to explore the many references, user forums and links, especially if you plan to create more books. The more you know about the process, the more comfortable you will become with it.

In this screen shot the arrows point to the two places that say **"SIGN UP."** Select either and it is an easy step by step process to sign up.

Again, there are no costs to being a member, no hidden fees, no "gottcha" tricks.

Also, **CS** does not send you unwanted emails or solicitations or bombard you with sales offers.

It really is a straightforward business for self-publishing.

Screen Shot to Opening a CS account.

Chapter 5:

Begin the 10 Steps

1. Go to Createspace
2. Log into your account
3. Start your title
4. Start your new project
5. Title information
6. ISBN
7. Interior Set up: Upload your book
8. Create your cover
9. Launch previewer
10. Review your book

   Make changes or Accept

   DONE !!!!!!!

   Now for the details.

Step by Step to Publish:

Let the arrows below guide you.

1. Go to Createspace.com:

2. Log in to your CS account:

3. Start a Title for Free:

Select the longer box "Start a title for free".

Notice the Publishing Advisor Tool for help on

this page. There is something like this on every

page. There are also many offers for paid

services. I have never used any paid service and

know nothing about them or their costs.

4. Start Your New Project:

You will use the screen below for the next 4 steps. I have reproduced smaller sections of it on the next few pages.

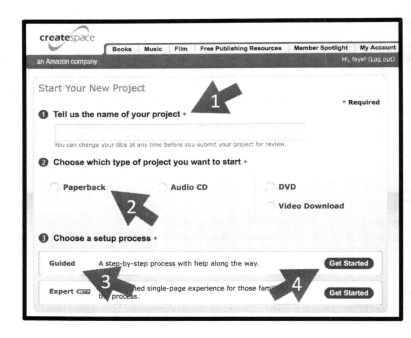

a. NAME OF YOUR PROJECT is the title of your book. You can modify or change your title at any time, so if not sure, make it up and change it later, so you can move forward.

b. Select **PAPERBACK**

c. Choose **GUIDED** set up.

The Guided set up option gives the best help to get a more detailed step by step process.

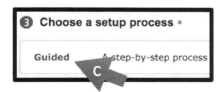

d. Select **GET STARTED**.

Guided A step-by-step process with help along the way.	**Get Started**

d

5. Title Information:

Title Information		◀ Back Next ▶

What to do on this page: Enter title information, including title and author. This information is associated with your book's ISBN and cannot be changed after you complete the review process.

* Required

Title * `Getting it Done` a

Subtitle
What's this?

Primary Author *
What's this?
Prefix   First Name / Initial   Middle Name / Initial   Last Name / Surname *   Suffix b

Add Contributors   `Authored by` ◆ **Add**
What's this?

☐ This book is part of a series (What's this?)

Series Title   Volume ◆

Edition number
What's this?

Language *   `English` ◆
What's this?

Publication Date
What's this?

Save   **Save & Continue**

Be sure and hit
Save & Continue
when done with page.

Fill in Boxes: (required items a. & b.)

a. **Title**: Mine is "Getting it Done."

Before you can print, this title and the title on the cover must be the same.

b. **Primary Author:** Write in any name or even a pseudonym.

c. **Subtitle**: If you have one, put it in.

d. **Add Contributors**:

Click on the arrows. You will see a LONG list of choices to include. I like to include my artist, although, I am not required or obligated to. If you have co-writers or editors or anyone you want to give recognition for helping you it can be done here. The screen shot on the next page lists suggestions from **CS**.

These are about half of the **CS** suggestions for contributors.

e. **Series Title:**

There is a small box that needs to be checked if you have a series you are writing.

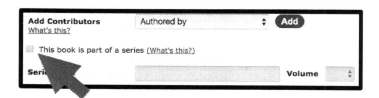

f. **Edition number:**

Leave blank unless you revise after publishing and have a 2nd published edition.

If this is the single book you plan to write, there is no series and no edition. You can always change this if you decide to write more books.

g. **Language:**

English (default), or to preferred language.

h. **Publication Date:**

Leave blank. **CS** will fill it in.

Save and Continue:

This step is **IMPORTANT** as it will preserve your hard work.

You will see a note "Working" to show your info is being saved.

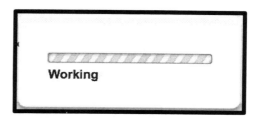

6. ISBN:

ISBN was introduced and explained on an earlier page, in Chapter 3 Intro to Book Covers. You are being asked if you want a free ISBN. I suggest you do it. The second screen shot shows what it looks like when it is issued, which takes only seconds.

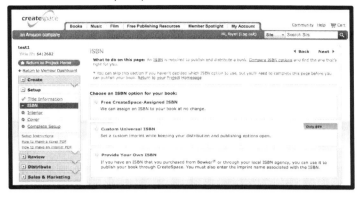

This is what it looks like after ISBN is issued.

REMEMBER TO CLICK CONTINUE

7. Interior Set Up

There are 3 items to select on the next screen,

Trim size, **Color** or **Black and White**, and

Paper color.

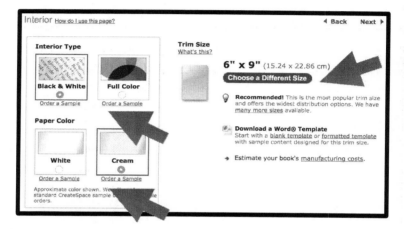

Select Trim Size:

If you typed your book in 8.5"X11", it will be easiest to choose this size. If you want to use a smaller size, pick the CHOOSE A DIFFERENT SIZE box. The screen shot shows 6" x9" being selected. Here is the list of the many **CS trim size** choices.

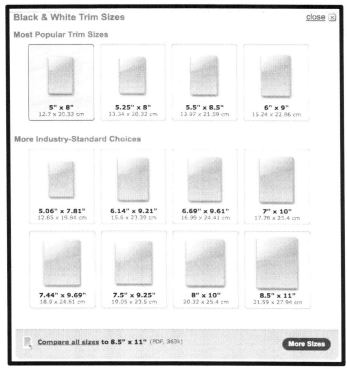

This "Step by Step" book is a 5"x 8" size.

Look carefully at the next screen in the 2nd paragraph it gives you an opportunity to download a Word Template and put your manuscript into the template.

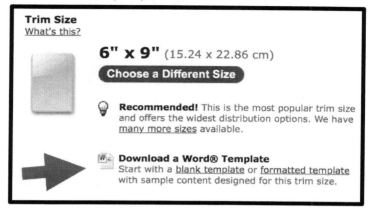

Download a Word Template:

If you want to use one of the templates you will need to download it and then open it from the download folder.

Select Black and White or Color:

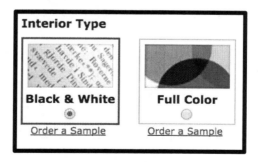

Select Paper Color:

You have a choice of white or cream.
You can order samples. Cream pages are
thicker. There is no cream choice
for the 8.5" x 11" book size.
The 10 Easy Steps book uses cream.

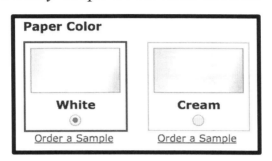

Upload your book file:

THIS IS IT! YOU ARE SENDING
YOUR BOOK TO BE PUBLISHED!

1. Select "**Upload Your Book File**".

Choose how you'd like to submit your interior:

⦿ Upload your Book File

2. SAVE

It is now time to choose the file name of your book. Find the correct name. Your book should be saved on your desktop. You will get one of the two screens below. They each ask you to select your book file. The file will come up from your computer when you click on "CHOOSE" or 'BROWSE'. Do not type anything in the space. Click on the correct name in your list of files, then select OPEN in the bottom right corner.

NOTE: If you have any trouble finding the correct file, use the search bar on the top right of the page and type in the correct file name. That will bring it up.

3. Choose File

The next screen will show CHOOSE FILE

REMEMBER TO SAVE!

REMEMBER TO SAVE!

The next screen shot is purposely sideways to make it as large as possible so you can read it.

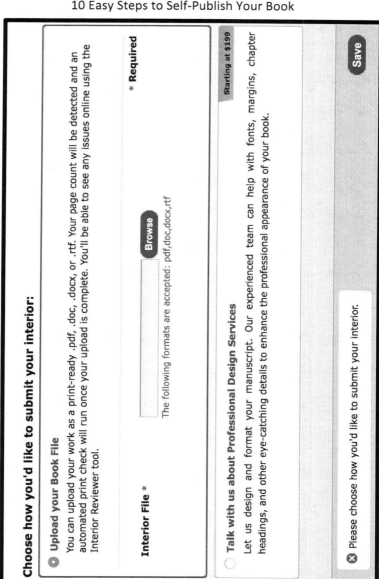

Choose how you'd like to submit your interior:

◉ Upload your Book File

You can upload your work as a print-ready .pdf, .doc, .docx, or .rtf. Your page count will be detected and an automated print check will run once your upload is complete. You'll be able to see any issues online using the Interior Reviewer tool.

Interior File *

* **Required**

Browse

The following formats are accepted: pdf,doc,docx,rtf

○ Talk with us about Professional Design Services
Starting at $199

Let us design and format your manuscript. Our experienced team can help with fonts, margins, chapter headings, and other eye-catching details to enhance the professional appearance of your book.

⊗ Please choose how you'd like to submit your interior.

Save

You Will See Your Files:

If you get the BROWSE screen. DO NOT
TYPE ANYTHING IN THE SEARCH BOX.
Your computer files will show on your screen.
Find the file that is your final book file that you
wrote down on a piece of paper. That is the file
to select and then select the word OPEN or the
word CHOOSE at the bottom right of the
screen. The name of your book will show up
automatically in the blank search area.

Name	Date Mod
YES WORDHow to Self 7/4 9pm .docx	Today, 8:
how to pub seminar SCREEN SHOTS	Today, 7:
Back of Book description.docx	Today, 4:
PUBLIC DOMAIN WEBSITES	Today, 3:
pub domain images.pages	Today, 3:
YES WORDHow to Self 7/4 9pm .pdf	Today, 1:
NO WORDHow to Self 7/3 11pm .docx	Today, 12
Screen Shot 2016-07-05 at 12.02.48 PM.png	Today, 12
Screen Shot 2016-07-05 at 9.07.06 AM.png	Today, 9:
BOOK SECTIONS	Today, 7:
Faye Generic	Today, 7:
TEST 1 HOW TO BOOK.docx	Yesterda
TEST 1 HOW TO BOOK.pdf	Yesterda
CLASS- HOW TO SELF PUBLISH	Jul 3, 20
how to group with word for MAC.png	Jul 2, 20
YES -How to Self 6/30 10pm 80 pgs .docx	Jun 30, 2
FINAL 1- self pub Beginning June 30 8X11 copy 2.pages	Jun 30, 2

Remember to click SAVE

at the bottom of the screen.

This screen shot shows what your screen will look like, (only it will list your files, not mine).

After you have uploaded your file next to the word BROWSE, hit SAVE.

You see how my book file is highlighted. I then hit OPEN which is at the bottom of the page.

Instead of the word OPEN you may have the word CHOOSE.

Find the correct book file. Select it so it highlights. At the bottom of the page click on OPEN.

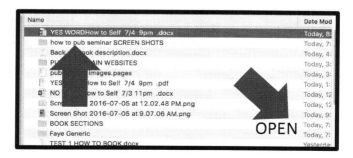

Your files will start to upload and you will see the words "WORKING", then "UPLOADING" and maybe "PROCESSING." It will show you the progress of the upload in %.

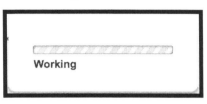

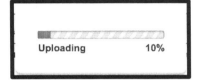

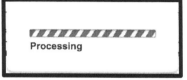

UPLOADING   **PROCESSING**

UPLOADING   40%

Select No Bleed

The bleed is how far the picture extends to the edge of the page. A full bleed means the picture goes to all edges with no margins.

If your book is primarily text, select a "non-bleed" format.

If you want full bleed, be sure to review carefully margin requirements. Every picture book I published was full bleed and had margin issues and I had to resubmit several times. Fortunately, it was only time consuming and **CS** was very helpful. It got resolved and the books look great.

Chapter 6:
Previewing Your Book

CS Runs an Interior Review

When the upload is complete, **CS** runs a check of your book files looking for problems. They do not check spelling or grammar. This may take 10 to 20 minutes. You will get a response from them like the one below. You will notice I had 7 issues with my uploaded book. So DO NOT WORRY if you get a message like this. It is common and not a big deal.

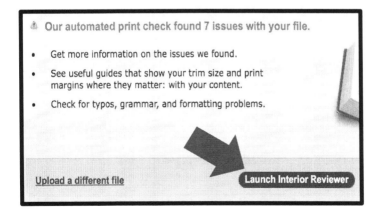

You need to

LAUNCH INTERIOR REVIEWER to see what the book looks like. It will take only a few seconds and then you can see your actual book and all of the issues **CS** has identified.

You will now be seeing exactly what your book will look like when printed. You can do this step before or after you have submitted your cover. It is recommended you make notes to yourself on what you need to change. Look for typos, and spacing and especially breaches of margins. You cannot make any changes on the **CS** copy. All changes have to be made in your original manuscript and resubmitted as a new file. Chapter 8 explains this in detail.

First you will see the top screen. Then the words "Get Started". Then the first page of your book. It is quite exciting.

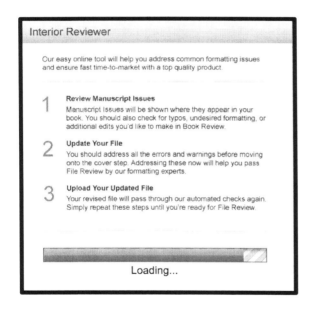

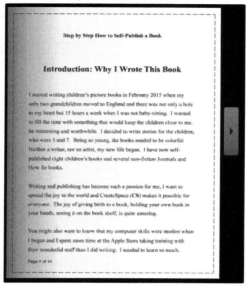

This is the **Launch Interior Reviewer** screenshot of the book you are now reading. You will see some of the issues listed for this book.

Taking a look at the different problems **CS** has found in my book, I confess these issues have been in all of my books, so let's assume they will be in yours as well.

Chapter 7: The Problems

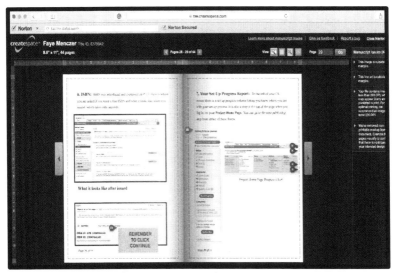

In this image of two pages there are two problems identified with 2 symbols.

This is the symbol for poor resolution of a picture, not enough DPI (dots per inch). When speaking to **CS** about the poor resolution issues they said that the PREVIWER is a low resolution tool and that it is difficult to tell how serious the problem is by looking at the preview book. It is only by seeing the actual PROOF of

75

the book that you will know if it is acceptable or not. Unless, it looks really terrible, I will let the low resolution go. **CS** will publish a low dpi book.

This means the text is into the margin and will be cut off, or come very close to the edge of the page. This is a serious issue and **CS** will not print the book. I write down what pages have to be fixed and correct them in my original file and then resubmit my NEW File (with a new name) and go through the publishing process again. This "*10 Easy Steps*" book I submitted for a preliminary review 5 or 6 times before I was satisfied enough to submit it for a final review and print it. Rewriting and resubmitting takes time and patience, but is also part of the challenge of the successful outcome.

CS lists problems with your book in two places.

They are listed on the actual page and on the sidebar called "Manuscript Issues"

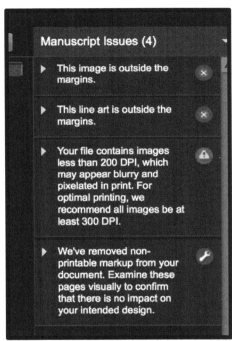

CS lists on the right side of your document the specific issues they found in your book and on the individual pages. The image on the next page demonstrates a useful tool. It provides a thumbnail view of all of the pages of your book and what the issues are. I find it especially helpful when I want to take notes on what pages need fixing.

Some Thumbnail pages of *10 Easy Steps*

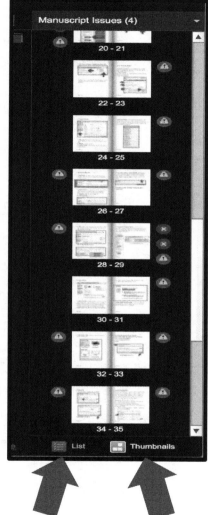

List mode   **Thumbnails mode**

The switch to change between "**Thumbnails**" and **"List"** mode is easy to miss so the arrows are pointing it out. The **"LIST"** is what is shown on a previous page.

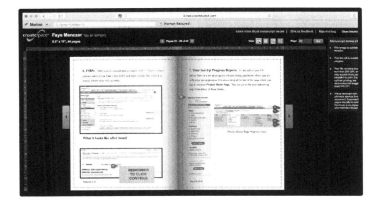

Here are more key elements to the Previewer page.

This is at the top of the document. You can go to whatever page you want by typing in the page number and click GO. You can enlarge the

picture, which is very helpful when look at

multiple pages using this icon .

Go Back and Make Changes Ignore Issues and Save

At the bottom of your Previewer is the choice to

GO BACK AND MAKE CHANGES or to

IGNORE ISSUES and SAVE (in red). If you

decide to ignore and save, you can always go

back and upload a new corrected file, especially

if the issues do not bother you. If the issues are

significant it is better to go back and make the

corrections.

When you have completed your preview of the

book, the last step is to **CLOSE INTERIOR**

REVIEWER which is located in the upper right

hand corner of screen.

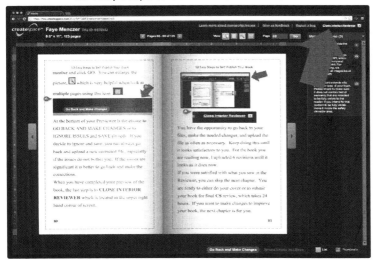

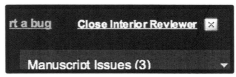

You have the opportunity to go back to your files, make the needed changes, and upload the file as often as necessary. Keep doing this until it looks satisfactory to you. For the book you are reading now, I uploaded 6 revisions until it looks as it does now.

If you were satisfied with what you saw in the Reviewer, you can skip the next chapter. You are ready to either do your cover or to submit your book for final **CS** review, which takes 24 hours. If you want to make changes to improve your book, the next chapter is for you.

Hired Help:

You can hire people to do any of the publishing process. CreateSpace lists its many publishing for fee services. Fiverr.com is another resource. There are many more on the web.

Chapter 8:

Revisions & Resubmitting

Every time you do a revision, after you have selected IGNORE ISSUES and SAVE, you will need to again go through the same submission process already detailed.

When resubmitting your new file and going through the different forms, most items **Do Not Need to Be Changed.** You should keep the same title, the same ISBN, the same size document.

When you correct your manuscript, and have a new PDF file to submit, I urge you to give it a **NEW FILE NAME**, that you have written down.

I strongly recommend you keep your old files of your book in a folder until you are absolutely sure you will not need them.

When the new file is ready to be uploaded, and you get back to this screen, select UPLOAD A DIFFERENT FILE. It is in small print in red ink and easy to miss. You are asked to upload it in two different places.

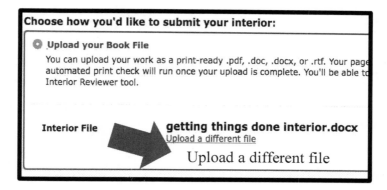

After it uploads, you again are asked go through the reviewing process and repeat all of the previous steps. and see if it looks satisfactory to you.

If you have completed your cover and that is also to your satisfaction you are ready to submit the book for CS to review. This takes about 24 hours. When you get the email that it has been reviewed, it will tell you any problems with the new book file. It is very prudent to again proof your book for issues before printing. The time spent looking over your book before the actual publishing is very important for catching errors, but you can still revise even after you have had your book printed.

10 Easy Steps had 3 printed revisions before all the errors were caught.   It is all part of the challenge of learning new skills.

If you have not yet created your book cover Chapter 9 will take you through that process.

Chapter 9: Creating Your Cover

You have two choices you can create your own cover using whatever program you are comfortable using or you can follow the **CS** template

---

IMPORTANT: Whichever choice you make, before submitting your final cover for review, the title on the cover of your book must be the same as the title listed on your Title Information (see p.53). If they are not the same, CS will not allow you to print your book.

Building Your Own Cover

Remember you need a front and back cover. If your book is 75 or more pages, like this one, you can also have text on the spine. Your cover can be all text or have a picture or photo or any art you choose. It is not possible to take you through the many choices for covers. I suggest you create what you like and is easiest for you.

Using Cover Creator:

If you have limited computer skills, you might find it easiest to use the **CS** cover templates. To use their covers, select Cover Creator tool and build your cover within **CS**. You will not be able to keep a copy of the cover in your files, if you use their Cover Creator, but that may not be important to you.

Whichever set up you use for your cover when you go back to your **CS Member Dashboard** you will need to click **COVER** on either of the two screens on the next two pages. The first one is from the **PROJECT HOME PAGE,** and is the **SET UP** section in cream below.

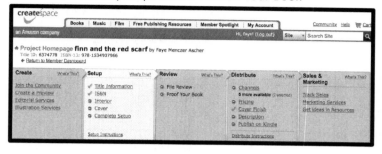

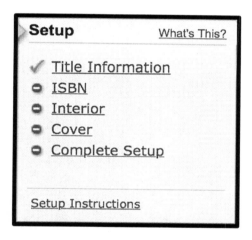

Select **COVER** on either of the screens shown. The next index is an enlarged view from the side bar of the screen where you list your PDF interior and cover files.

If you are doing your own cover the next display is the screen shot of how you choose to up load

your own file. The top line is to BUILD YOUR COVER ONLINE using templates from **CS** to design the cover. The bottom choice is if you have already designed your cover, have saved it as a PDF and are ready to upload it to **CS**.

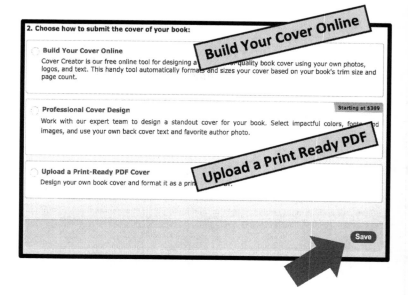

Which ever you choose be sure to SAVE at the bottom of the page.

Using CS Cover Creator

CS cover creator offers you many choices of cover styles and themes.

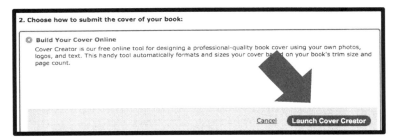

The first step is to **Launch Cover Creator.**

After you choose **Launch Cover Creator** this screen will appear. The green circles show what you have completed.

As you go through each item **CS** gives clear directions of what to do. You can play around and have fun looking at different possibilities. Let's go through the items one task at a time.

Theme: This is the layout look for your covers.

There are several choices.

Whatever theme you select there are very few changes you can make in font, position of text, text size, or other items. At the bottom of the chart is **CHANGE DESIGN.** Selecting that will allow you to change the theme and design of the whole cover.

In this Task List the theme selected is **Traditions.** When you have the theme you want, click **NEXT.**

Title: It will appear in the same position, font and size that you see in the example.

Subtitle: One thing to keep in mind is being careful of trying to alter spacing of text with the space bar. It will make your title smaller, but not shift its position on the page. You can't alter placement. On this book I could not figure out why both the titles "Getting Things Done" and "Keeping Promises to Myself" were so small.

CS researched the problem and told me it was my hitting the space bar and reducing the space for the text.

Author: You can place your name or use this line for other text, having nothing to do with your name.

Front Cover Image: If you want art on the cover you **MUST** select an image of some kind. You do not automatically get the image you see in the theme. You need to pick some background or you will get plain white. If you prefer a plain cover, no art, you have that option, and a choice of colors or designs.

ALERT: CS has had some problems with the cover creator. If there are glitches, call CS and they will let you know if the problem is from their end. Call sooner, before you get too stressed.

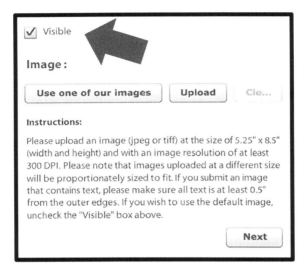

The choice of "**VISIBLE**" is offered to you in different places for the cover. If you want **no** picture, only text, **UNCHECK** the box.

There is a range of art you can use, including your own photos or graphics. If you want to **use your own** art or photo click the UPLOAD.

Then go to your personal photos file and select the photo you want and upload it to the cover. Also notice if the picture in the theme flows over the front and the back of the book or only does one cover. Your selected art must comply.

To use a **CS** image from their files, click this option.

CS offers many choices of images. The list at the top of the next page is only a partial inventory of subjects. Each subject has a catalog of pictures. Click on the different items to see your options.

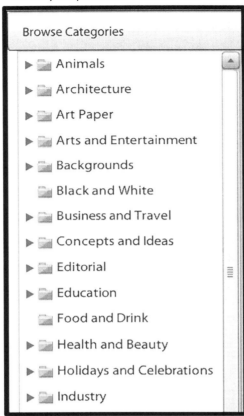

REMEMBER TO CLICK NEXT at the bottom right of

page when you are ready to move to the next subject.

Author photo: Upload your favorite selfie or

uncheck visible if you want to leave it blank.

TIP: At the top of the front cover screen are some important choices you can make.

If you want to get rid of frames around your photo or you have no photo and the frame is still there click **HIDE FRAMES.** The frames are just a reference for the photo edges or text box edges. They do not print.

 These items are size viewing modes to evaluate your cover. They do not change your images or text layout. The box with the arrows will fit the cover to your screen window. The 100% is a 1 - 1 dot representation of your cover, and the 200% doubles the size.

If you are proof reading your text before submitting, try using 200% to see the text more clearly

Publisher logo: Create one, or uncheck **visible** and leave blank.

Back cover text: Describe what your book is about or you can leave it entirely blank of text and only have the wrapped picture showing. The next screen shot is of one of my books and it shows both covers. On the left is the back cover. You can see the description text box, the place for the photo, in the upper left circle. The small rectangle in lower left is for your logo and the bigger bottom rectangle is where **CS** automatically places your ISBN. You can experiment with the cover and see different options.

Background color: Many choices. Different themes have different options.

Font color: Same as above.

When you have completed all of the steps, click **Submit Cover.**

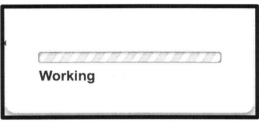

Working

You will see this screen and know your cover is being uploaded and saved.

The cover artwork on p.100 is an image from **CS** Cover Creator files.

On the final cover I created, I unchecked visual for photo and logo, so they do not show.

Chapter 10: Completing Book

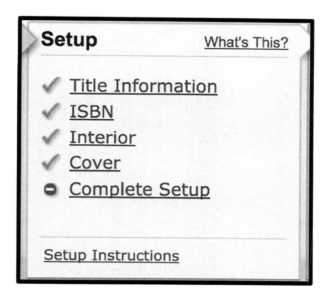

Almost done. There are only a few more forms to fill in. The next stage is the "DISTRIBUTE" selections.

You need to fill in something in these areas even if you are not planning to sell

Distribute

✓ Cover Finish

⊖ Description

⊖ Channels

⊖ Pricing

⊖ Publish on Kindle

Save Progress

Complete

Distribute:

Cover finish: Select Matte or Glossy

Description: CS requires you to put something here to describe your book. It can be minimal.

BISAC: Select a category that is closest to the subject of your book. If no category fits select **non-classifiable**.

If you don't plan to market your book, SELECT NONE OF THE DISTRIBUTION CHOICES.

Channels: These are the channels of distribution. If you don't want to publicly promote your book, do not select any channels. Channels also affect your cost and pricing.

Author biography: You are required to write something.

Language: English (or whatever it is)

Country of publication: United States

Search keywords: Put in anything applicable

Contains adult content: Check this box if it applies

Large print: Choose if you want this

Publish on Kindle: After publishing your hard copy it is easy to create an E-book on Kindle.

104

Pricing: You must select a price that is at least the price that **CS** lists as the minimum. Even if you don't plan to market and promote your book as a commercial venture CS requires you to select a price to sell it to others, and for your author price.

Submit your files for review: CS will look over your book and send you an email about your files . You now can go to Launch Previewer and see what the specific issues with your book are.

CS will advise you of the problems, if any, and you can make changes, and go through the process again, or ignore the issues and SAVE. If the issues are serious **CS** may not allow you to print. If minor you can order a proof.

Reviewer. If you like how it looks order a proof to see the book in print. This is very important. Several times I caught glaring spelling or editing errors with the physical book that I did not catch the zillion times I looked over my manuscript or the PREVIEW book. Before you order copies for your loved ones, you want it to be right.

At any time you can make changes to the all of the above choices.

Order a PROOF: It takes 7-10 days for the proof to come. Get out the celebration beverages. After the celebration look the proof over carefully. CS recommends you follow the list on the next page.

You will get a message like this after ordering.

ORDER: Your proof has shipped.
Please review your proof carefully, as
CS prints exactly as submitted.

THE FINAL STEP IS TO APPROVE THE PROOF AND ORDER YOUR BOOKS.

Approve Proof

Please carefully review your printed proof for formatting, grammar, and design corrected. We recommend using the following guidelines when reviewing your p

Review your book three times, with each time focusing on a different aspect. If you try to review all of this information in one sitting, you could miss something.

- The first time: Check the format, including headers/footers, page numbers, spacing, table of contents and index.

- The second time: Review any images or graphics, and captions if applicable.

- The third time: Read the book for grammatical errors and/or typos.

Pay special attention to anything that we fixed for you (e.g. extending bleed or shifting margins) to ensure that the work meets your expectations

Get an objective perspective. Have someone unfamiliar with your book read it thoroughly.

Click on **CALCULATE.** After a few seconds a price will appear in the blue box. This is the minimum the book can be sold for.

Your Price: Orders you place for your own title are referred to as "Member Orders." When you order copies of your own book, you pay just the fixed and per-page charges plus shipping and handling. Use **CS** calculators to see your per-book, proof order cost, and shipping and handling costs.

What Will You Pay?

To find out your costs do the following steps:

Go to Member Dashboard

Select BOOKS

Select PUBLISH TRADE PAPERBACKS

Select BUYING COPIES

Near the bottom of the buying copies page is the **Member Order Calculator.**

FILL IN - Interior Type, Trim Size, Number of Pages and Quantity. (if not already listed)

Click on **CALCULATE**.

After a few seconds a price will appear in the window that **CS** has calculated for you. Do the same thing with **Order Shipping Calculator.**

I found that 10 books were cheaper, and a better value per book, than buying one, the shipping was also less per book, the more I ordered.

Changing Your Book:

If you upload new files, after your book has been reviewed by **CS** your book will be submitted for review and again take 24 hours. But it is worth the wait to make sure the book looks the way you want it to.

Anytime you do not understand what to do about an error or a problem, call **CS**. I can't stress enough how helpful and cooperative they are.

Ordering Author Copies:

Once you have approved the proof of your physical book, you may order as many "author copies" at the author price you wish. Remember, you can make whatever changes you think necessary even after the book has been printed and available.

> **YOU HAVE COMPLETED THE SELF PUBLISHING PROCESS. CONGRATULATIONS. BE PROUD, AS A NEW PARENT.**

Conclusion:

Phone Numbers and Websites

It is impossible to cover all issues so I hope this list will be helpful to you.

APPLE: 1-800-275-2273
CREATESPACE: 1-866-356-2154
MS WORD: 1-877-696-7786

FIVERR.COM: Freelance contractors from around the world who do everything and prices begin at $5. I have only used my picture book artist, Phanminhtuan, whom I have never met or spoken to and lives in Vietnam. He has done 6 books for me and is great.

PUBLIC DOMAIN PHOTOS/ART:

http//:www.pdpiCS.com

http//:www.photopublicdomain.com

http//:www.mypublicdomainpictures.com

Dear Reader,

This book is at its end and I hope it has been helpful to you and you have successfully published your book. Hearing about your writing and publishing experience would really please me. So if you have an extra few minutes won't you please send me an email (bubbiepublishing@gmail.com) and let me know about your adventures with your book? Include a screen shot of your cover. I really care about you and your efforts.

Faye Menczer Ascher

Other Books by *Faye Menczer Ascher*

Keeping Promises to Myself Series

☀My Self-Publishing Journal

☀Getting It Done Journal

☀10 Easy Steps to Self Publishing

EMILY and FINN Series

☀Playing All Day Long

☀We Love Trains

☀The Red Scarf: Things Just Happen

HOW THE ANIMAL GETS ITS... Series

☀How the Zebra Gets Her Stripes

☀How the Snail Gets Its Shell

☀How the Elephant Gets Its Ears

☀How the Camel Gets Its Hump

Kindle E-Books

☀A to Z Knock Knock Jokes

NOTES:

NOTES:

Made in the USA
Charleston, SC
22 October 2016